Guinea Pigs

Carolyn Ruf

t.f.h.

Special thanks for their special help with this book go to Alan and Linda Oberle, the A.C.B.A. and A.R.B.A., Susan Ball, Peanut Butter, and Ceci.

© 1990 by T.F.H. Publications, Inc. Ltd.

Distributed in the UNITED STATES by T.F.H. Publications, Inc., One T.F.H. Plaza, Neptune City, NJ 07753; in CANADA to the Pet Trade by H & L Pet Supplies Inc., 27 Kingston Crescent, Kitchener, Ontario N2B 2T6; Rolf C. Hagen Ltd., 3225 Sartelon Street, Montreal 382 Quebec; in CANADA to the Book Trade by Macmillan of Canada (A Division of Canada Publishing Corporation), 164 Commander Boulevard, Agincourt, Ontario M1S 3C7; in ENGLAND by T.F.H. Publications Limited, Cliveden House/Priors Way/Bray, Maidenhead, Berkshire SL6 2HP, England; in AUSTRALIA AND THE SOUTH PACIFIC by T.F.H. (Australia) Pty. Ltd., Box 149, Brookvale 2100 N.S.W., Australia; in NEW ZEALAND by Ross Haines & Son, Ltd., 82 D Elizabeth Knox Place, Panmure, Auckland, New Zealand; in the PHILIPPINES by Bio-Research, 5 Lippay Street, San Lorenzo Village, Makati Rizal; in SOUTH AFRICA by Multipet Pty. Ltd., Box 235 New Germany, South Africa 3620. Published by T.F.H. Publications, Inc. Manufactured in the United States of America by T.F.H. Publications, Inc.

Contents

Photography: Dr. Herbert R. Axelrod, Michael Gilroy, Isabelle Francais, Brian Seed, Louise Van der Meid.

Line illustrations by Ross A. Norris and Miss P. Swanborough.

The Perfect Pet Pig

Our guinea pigs are one of the world's best pets! A good pet is gentle, attentive, and affectionate. Also, for us a good pet is one for which it is easy to provide care and food. The pet provides us with responsibility and enjoyment.

The guinea pig should never have been overlooked as a popular pet for anyone. So many folks opt for a dog or cat whether their time, budget, or lifestyle is suitable or not! It seems many people are mismatched with a pet or are petless because they have not considered one of the small mammals—the little guys.

The small mammal category includes mice, gerbils, hamsters, domestic rats, guinea pigs, and rabbits. The guinea pig is right in the middle of the small mammal size spectrum.

Guinea pigs are a good size to handle and have one obvious popular advantage, especially if you or your mother is squeamish about almost hairless, rat-like tails: the guinea pig is tailless. The other small mammals have perfectly nice tails, but our little pig has none. So, we can discard the old saying, "If you pick up a guinea pig by its tail, its eyes will pop out." What an awful thing to say anyway! For some reason not yet disclosed, our little *Cavia porcellus* (that is Latin for guinea pig—pretty fancy) is the only domestic rodent that is tailless.

At the other end, guinea pigs are the most vocal of the small mammals. They whistle, wheep, squeap, purr, chatter, and make parakeet-like sounds. They endear themselves to their owner, who is convinced the guinea pig is responding to them. And, you know, that is usually true. The more time you spend with any pet, the better you will know him or her and he will know you. The more attention the pet gets, the more its personality will blossom.

Why has the general public relegated the guinea pig to the ranks of a children's pet? It is true the guinea pig is an excellent pet for a child, but it is also an excellent pet for an adult! Consider those things that make them good children's pals. They are hand-size; they rarely bite; they respond (often loudly) to their owner; they take up little room; they are inexpensive to feed and house. Shall I go on? That's what the rest of this book is for—going on about guinea pigs.

The Guinea Pig as a Pet

What is a Guinea Pig?

The guinea pig is a misnamed animal. A guinea pig is not a pig. Neither is it from Guinea. The guinea pig is a member of the rodent family. It is the only domestic rodent without a tail. Its more proper name is cavy (rhymes with gravy). Professional breeders and people who show guinea pigs usually call them cavies.

Let's take a look at the peculiar origin of the guinea pig's name. The short, stout shape and mealtime squeals may be similar to a pig's shape and sounds. That may explain the "pig." Male guinea pigs are called boars, the females are called sows. However, the young are called pups, not piglets!

"Guinea" may come from the archaic meaning of the word, which was "foreign." Guinea pigs came from South America, so the English may have dubbed them "foreign pigs" or guinea pigs. Another possibility is that guinea is a corruption of Guiana, the South American region from which guinea pigs were exported. Europeans may also have thought that the animals came from the West African coast of Guinea, since they were imported from South America via the Guinea slave trade ships. The last possibility is that guinea pigs were sold for one guinea (a gold coin worth 21 shillings) a piece in England.

The guinea pig, or cavy, is a rodent closely related to the chinchilla. They are both in the group of rodents called hystricomorphs. This group also includes the acouchi, agouti, coypu, cuis, plains viscacha, tuco-tuco. and wild guinea pig! These are all South American residents.

The wild guinea pig, *Cavia cutleri*, is the ancestor of our pet guinea pig. It is dark-furred and a bit smaller than the domestic guinea pig, *Cavia porcellus*. It lives in the Brazilian grasslands, treeless plains or pampas of Argentina, and foothills of Peru. Wild guinea pigs are vegetarians like our pet guinea pigs. They are also diurnal, which means they are active in the daytime. Most domestic guinea pigs are active in the nighttime as well, but take a nap in the afternoon. The native Indians of Peru use wild guinea pigs for meat and consider them a delicacy. Some ancient chieftains even wore wild cavy furs.

Guinea pigs made their entrance into European circles via the 16th century Spaniards, who imported them from South America. In Europe they became popular as pets. Queen Elizabeth I helped to contribute to this pet fancy. At one

The Guinea Pig as a Pet

time, the guinea pig might be found substituted for the more familiar dog or cat in family portraits. Certain religious paintings of that time even show the Christ Child visited by the three Magi, a rabbit, and a guinea pig!

The guinea pig has been repeatedly described as "shaped like a brick with the corners chopped off." No guinea pig book would be complete without that adage. The blunt-nosed, short-eared guinea pig may indeed resemble a carved brick. Some guinea pigs are likened to wigs, mops, and short-eared rabbits. Whatever the comparison, guinea pigs are charming creatures and pets.

Should You Have a Pet?

Why do people have pets? We have them for companionship, for protection, for someone to care for, to have someone who will love us no matter what mistakes we made that day. We have pets because we enjoy and appreciate their beauty, their behavior, and their trusting natures. There are many candidates for pets, but there are also many considerations before making a final selection.

Before a decision is made on a pet, every future pet owner should:

1. Make a list of the characteristics hoped for in the pet, and

2. Make an evaluation of his lifestyle and its suitability to favorably accommodate a pet.

Failure to honestly assess the particular animal and one's willingness to devote time, money, and patience to the animal will cause unnecessary and avoidable unhappiness, annoyance, and emotional strain on the pet and the owner.

Your decision when selecting a pet should reveal maturity on your part and a long-term commitment to the animal. To be fair to the pet, you and your family or friends, if you are living with others, must frankly answer several questions. The key to a happy association with you and your new pet is compatibility and responsibility.

The Peruvian and Silkie guinea pigs require more coat care than other varieties.

1. Do you have time to care properly for a pet?

2. What size pet will comfortably

The Guinea Pig as a Pet

fit your home and your pocketbook? Are you prepared for possible veterinary expenses for vaccinations, neutering, and illnesses?

3. Are you allergic to any animals? Shedding fur can be a household nuisance, and the dander associated with it is an irritant to many human allergies. Also, grooming a long-haired dog or guinea pig (!) is time consuming and requires patience.

4. Is a young or adult animal more appropriate for your situation? The personality of an adult is already developed, so you know what he is like. You can help shape the personality of a youngster, however. Young animals, of course, are not yet trained in proper etiquette and require much attention, time, and patient training.

5. Why do you really want a pet?

6. Is that a sound reason to take on the responsibility of a living thing?

7. Do you want a male or a female? Is it better to have a single animal or a couple? This depends on the kind of animal. Caged animals (like guinea pigs) may be happier with a friend. To prevent litters there should be two of the same sex. Familiarize yourself with the animal's characteristics to learn whether two males will fight and if a single pet can be kept happily.

8. Are you allowed and able to keep a pet where you live?

9. Who will be responsible for the care and feeding of the pet? The duties should be delegated and accepted before the pet's adoption.

10. Are you willing to give the pet a lot of attention and time?

After these considerations have been discussed and handled, if it seems a pet is in store for you, you have the delightful task of selecting an appropriate pet.

Why a Guinea Pig?

That is one of my favorite questions. It provides the opportunity to brag about how delightful guinea pigs are as companions. Also, it gives me the chance to expound on how smart my own guinea pigs are.

Why would one purposely select a guinea pig for a pet? For you dog-lovers, I realize guinea pigs do not fetch newspapers or sticks, nor do they protect the house. They do, however, respond vocally and enthusiastically to their owner. They will run up to the edge of the cage, poke their nose up toward their friend, even stand on the hind feet, and whistle a loud "hello!".

For cat lovers who enjoy a purring cat in their lap, guinea pigs

Choosing a Pet Guinea Pig

will settle in your lap and purr in their own inimitable way. Their drawback is that they cannot be housebroken and may leave you a little wet. Nonetheless, they will chatter happily when held and sometimes even lick their human friend with little cavy kisses.

For pet owners who like a pet that is easy to care for, guinea pigs are perfect. They are fairly inexpensive, their food is not costly, and their housing is suitable for a small house or apartment. Guinea pigs do not require vaccinations for diseases like distemper or rabies, as dogs and cats do. They do not have to be licensed either.

Do they sound too good to be true? Visit a few friends who have guinea pigs. Take a trip to a county agricultural fair and take in the cavy show. If you are destined to be a guinea pig owner, you will be enthusiastic about your visits and ready to tackle the responsibility and fun of living with *Cavia porcellus*—the guinea pig!

The mother guinea pig is a good parent.

Now that you have decided a guinea pig is the type of pet you want, you have two more choices to make. One is what kind of guinea pig, and second, of course, is which individual guinea pig is going to share its life with you. There are several different kinds of guinea pigs, and each can be shown in cavy (guinea pig) shows. Each breed is recognized by the American Cavy Breeders Association and the American Rabbit Breeders Association. The American Cavy Breeders Association is a specialty club that promotes the guinea pig as a breed.

The American Rabbit Breeders Association publishes a *Standard of Perfection* book for rabbits and cavies. The standards are presented as the ideals that are selected for showing and breeding. *Standard of Perfection* covers type, fur, color, markings, and condition of the guinea pig. It has an excellent list of general faults and disqualifications, which is interesting in itself and necessary to know if you show your guinea pig friend. The *Standard of Perfection* can be ordered from the American Rabbit Breeders Association.

Here is the parade of the seven guinea pig breeds! Each one is

Choosing a Pet Guinea Pig

appealing with its particular special qualities.

Breeds

THE AMERICAN

The American is the most common guinea pig. It is calm and quite content to sit with anyone. Its short, silky hair comes in many colors and requires minimal grooming to remove dead hairs. They usually weigh a bit over two pounds. Some may weigh as much as three and a half pounds!

Americans come in 36 colors (counting all possible combinations). Guinea pigs are shown in one of 32 color groups. These are divided into Agoutis, Marked, Selfs, and Solids.

American guinea pigs have broad shoulders, a Roman nose, and a high full crown, which is the rounded bulge above the neck and shoulders in guinea pigs. They have large bright eyes that should match the body color, as should the feet in a show guinea pig. The ears should be slightly droopy.

These are your most common guinea pigs. The color, markings, etc., in the *Standard of Perfection* must be followed for showing a guinea pig. A *pet* guinea pig could be blue with red eyes and still make a marvelous pet. It would not be accepted as a fine quality American, but its friendly nature would qualify it well as a pet.

THE ABYSSINIAN

Abyssinians have short, harsh fur arranged in rosettes and ridges. Rosettes are circular cowlicks that radiate from one central point. Ideally Abyssinians should display four rosettes around the hips, four over the back as a saddle, and one or two on each shoulder. Each rosette should be round and should not overlap another. Abyssinians also sport a ruff, or collar, around the neck and a back ridge.

These are often the smallest and rangiest of the guinea pigs. They usually weigh 30 to 34 ounces, or an average of two pounds. This varies with the strain or breeding stock. Some people have Abyssinians who tip the scales at three and a half pounds!

The Abyssinian's nose is longer than the other guinea pigs'. They have a well-developed "moustache," which is actually ridges of hair along the cheeks. The eyes tend to be less round and less pronounced than in other breeds. Their little ears stick out sideways like little wings (at least compared to the other guinea pigs'

Choosing a Pet Guinea Pig

ears). They can be shown in the colors listed under Agouti, Marked, Self, and Solid coats.

They bear the distinction of being the most high strung or spirited. Because of their temperament, Abyssinians are allowed to move in a cavy show rather than be made to sit still. Actually, trying to pose an Abyssinian can be difficult.

Abyssinians are the most likely to demand food in their high-whistled voices, to struggle to be put down if held, snatch their feet away if they are being touched, and complain if patted on the chin. They are independent in an endearing way. By the way, they are my favorites.

THE PERUVIAN

The long-haired Peruvian is the most spectacular guinea pig. Their well-groomed coats can reach lengths of 12 to 14 inches or more! The Peruvian is judged primarily on this mane. The density of the coat and the sweeps of hair to the sides, rear, and over the head constitute the focus of attention. These mop-like guinea pigs, occasionally mistaken for wigs, can be Agouti, Marked, Self, or Solid colors. The colors tend to be lighter in long-haired Peruvians and Silkies.

A Peruvian's owner has to endure comments about his prized pet such as "How do you know which end is which?" or "He looks like a wind-up mop running across the room!" Never mind this; your Peruvian will provide a lot of companionship and enjoyment. But they are a big responsibility, and perhaps one should choose a different breed for the first guinea pig.

Peruvians need attentive grooming and bathing. My Peruvian never grew hair longer than 4 inches, and her companion nibbled her hair occasionally, too. I cut my Peruvian's hair when it became matted behind her rear legs. My Peruvian breeder friends will be aghast at that approach to hair care. The conscientious owner who is showing the Peruvian must check his Peruvian's hair daily and probably bathe the hindquarters, at least when the hair becomes soiled. The guinea pig's hair should be combed out at least every few days. If the hair is rolled up on tissue and fastened with rubber bands, it will stay beautiful more easily.

THE SILKIE

The Silkie is the other long-haired guinea pig. Its hair grows straight back to the rear with no part. The Silkie's shape, seen from above, is like a teardrop. It is very similar to the Peruvian.

Choosing a Pet Guinea Pig

THE TEDDY

The Teddy has an unusual short, kinky coat that is about half an inch long. This is a fairly new breed. The coat reminds you of a teddy bear.

THE WHITE CRESTED

The White Crested looks like an American, except it has a single white rosette. This rosette is set like a cap on top of the head just in front of the ears. Like the American, the Crested is a very calm guinea pig. Right now White Crested guinea pigs cannot be shown with any other white on them besides the single white rosette.

THE SATIN

The Satin is the newest recognized guinea pig breed. It resembles the American and White Crested. Its outstanding feature is its satin-like coat. The hair shaft is actually smaller and has a glass-like hair shell that reflects light. The result is a beautiful satiny sheen. The Satin guinea pig was first shown in 1981 and required two more convention showings and wide distributions across the United States to be accepted by the American Rabbit Breeders Association and the American Cavy Breeders Association. It is now recognized as a breed.

Color Varieties

Guinea pigs come in many colors and combinations of colors. They are divided into four groups: Agoutis, Marked, Selfs, and Solids. Each group contains a number of colors, as follows:

Agouti group:	Dilute, Golden, Silver
Marked group:	Broken Color, Dalmatian, Dutch, Himalayan, Tortoise Shell, Tortoise Shell and White
Self group:	Beige, Black, Blue, Chocolate, Cream, Lilac, Red, Red-eyed Orange, White
Solid group:	Brindle, Dilute, Golden, Roan, Silver

Guinea pigs with coats having hair shafts of two colors are agoutis. The color combinations can be from this list:

Base color:	Beige, Black, Chocolate, Lilac
Tip color:	Cream, Orange, Red, White

AGOUTIS

The agouti is a South American rodent closely related to our domestic guinea pig. The agouti color in the guinea pig resembles the wild agouti's coat. Each hair shaft has two bands of color. The guinea pig then has a base color with another color on the tip. The belly is the same color as the tip color. Agoutis also usually have black ticking (caused by black-tipped guard hairs), although the ticking should match the base color. Agoutis are divided into three groups that total 16 color combinations. For some reason, it is difficult to get a good shape on short-haired Agoutis.

Golden: The Golden Agouti has a blue-black base color with red tips. The coat has black ticking. The result is a beautiful golden chestnut color.

Silver: The Silver Agouti appears silver-white. Its base color or undercoat is blue-black with white tips. The coat has black ticking caused by the black guard hairs.

Dilute: The Dilute Agouti can be one of 14 color combinations. The base color may be beige, black, chocolate, or lilac. The tip color may be cream, orange, red, or white. So a dilute could be beige with cream tips on the hairs, beige with orange, beige with red, beige with white, etc. If you do your math correctly, you will discover 16 combinations if you include the Golden and Silver Agoutis.

MARKED

The Marked colored guinea pigs have two or more colors. They are the pintos and appaloosas of the guinea pig world. White Crested guinea pigs may be shown in the Marked category only as Tortoise Shell and Broken Color (without white).

Broken Color: A Broken Color is composed of any two or more recognized colors listed under Agouti, Self, and Solid. They cannot be any of the Marked colors like Himalayan or Tortoise Shell. At least one of the colors is arranged in patches. There is equal importance placed on the patches and their distribution. The patches should be sharp, clean, and not mixing. At least two of the patches must be the size of a 50-cent piece or bigger. The patches should be evenly distributed over the guinea pig.

If a guinea pig is allowed to graze outdoors it must be supervised continually.

Choosing a Pet Guinea Pig

Dalmatian: The Dalmatian, of course, is a spotted guinea pig. The spots can be of any one color on a white background. The spots should be distributed over much of the body. The head may be one of the Self colors (beige, black, blue, chocolate, cream, lilac, red, or white) or roaned (that is a color mixed with white hairs), and with a blaze. The feet and ears ideally should be the same color as the spots. The eyes are usually a deep ruby red.

Dutch: Like the Dutch rabbit, the Dutch guinea pig is a single color with a white belt around the neck and shoulders, white feet, and a white blaze. Dutch guinea pigs may be either a Self color or Agouti with the white markings. The markings should be very clear and distinct, giving a rather "dressed-up" look to the guinea pig.

Himalayan: The Himalayan color (also available in cats and rabbits) is as white as possible with rich black ears, muzzle, and feet. The pink eyes offset the dark ears and snout. The black color on the feet should run up as high as possible, like socks.

Tortoise Shell: This color is made up of patches of deep red and black. Ideally the patches should be arranged like a checkerboard. The patches should not be brindled (mixed with colored hairs) or overlapping.

Tortoise Shell and White: This is composed of patches of red, black, and white. Ideally these patches alternate from one side to the other. There should be a clear dividing line right down the middle of the back and the belly. To be shown as a Tortoise Shell or Tortoise Shell and White, the guinea pig must have at least one patch of each color that is the size of a 50-cent piece.

SELFS

Selfs are all one color all over. They may be beige, blue, chocolate, cream, lilac, red-eyed orange, red, or white. The eye colors frequently match the body color. For instance, black eyes for a black guinea pig, dark blue for a blue guinea pig, pink eyes for the beige. For some reason lilac and beige guinea pigs can be more aggressive toward people and often tend to nip.

SOLIDS

The Solids are mixed hair colors over the whole body.

Brindle: The Brindle color is an even mixture of black and red hairs. There should not be any patches, but a real mix.

Dilute: The Dilute is basically the same as the Dilute Agouti. The Agouti has a hair shaft of two

Choosing a Pet Guinea Pig

colors. The Dilute Solid has ticking that covers the whole body. In the Agouti, the belly is not ticked. The eyes of the Dilute are the same color as the base color.

Golden: The Golden, like the Golden Agouti, is a rich chestnut color. The hair tips are red and the base color is black. The black ticking covers the whole guinea pig, and the eyes are dark.

Silver: The Silver is a bright silver-white color caused by white-tipped hairs on a blue-black base. The black ticking covers the whole animal. The eyes should be a dark reddish color.

Roan: The Roans are a mixture of white and one or more colors. Usually they have Self colored heads (see under Selfs) and begin to roan out starting at the shoulders. They may have the same Self colored patches on their body and feet. Guinea pigs with the least number of patches are preferred in guinea pig shows. The toenails can be the color of any of the roaning colors on the guinea pig. White Crested guinea pigs may not be shown if they are roans.

There is the smorgasbord of guinea pigs from which you may choose, but it may be that you have already set eyes on the guinea pig you want. It may be a beautiful show quality animal like one described in the Breeds and Color Varieties sections, it may be an appealing animal in a pet store, or it might be one for which a friend must find a home. Either way, the guinea pig must appeal to *you.*

Please, when you select a potential pet, make sure it is healthy. Suppress the desire to help the runt, a sick or weak one, and choose one that is robust and healthy. You will be happier in the long run. The healthy individual is less likely to have problems or spread disease to other guinea pigs you may have.

Your new guinea pig should look well fed and alert. It also should have bright eyes and a dry nose. The coat should be full and have a healthy shine. Start out with a bright, healthy animal and you will probably have a long problem-free relationship with your new pet.

The feet of this Himalayan aren't visible, but if they were they would have to be black.

15

Feeding

A happy cavy is a healthy cavy. Good health is a result of being fed good food (among other things), but proper eating habits are one of the basics for good health also. Let us survey what our guinea pigs do eat, should eat, and from what they eat: the dinner and the dinnerware.

First of all, guinea pigs are herbivores or plant eaters. In the wild the little South American cavies graze on wild grasses and other vegetation. Our domestic guinea pigs rely on their owners to feed them the right foods. The main diet consists of guinea pig pellets. These can be bought at a feed or grain store or a pet store. Feeding a guinea pig is really inexpensive. Pellets may be bought in bulk for breeders who have many animals. Owners of only a few guinea pigs will probably buy a five-, ten-, or 25-pound bag.

Guinea pigs should eat fresh guinea pig pellets, not rabbit pellets. Now this is a surprise to many of you. Rabbit pellets are different from guinea pig pellets. One thing they don't have is vitamin C.

Below: Once your pet guinea pig gets used to you, it will enjoy eating from your hand.

16

If you plan to get more than one guinea pig, be sure to choose compatible animals. In most cases, males cannot be kept together.

Opposite top: The guinea pig has often been described as being shaped "like a brick with the corners chopped off." Opposite bottom: Juvenile Self Lilac guinea pigs are born darker than their parents. Above: A show quality Tortoise Shell and White Abyssinian boar.

Above: *A Marked boar with its young. Note the similarity of the blazes on these cavies.*
Opposite: *Show quality Golden White Crested sow.*

Opposite: *Longhaired guinea pig. A nutritious diet is imperative for the good health of your pet.* **Above:** *If cared for properly and handled often, your guinea pig will provide you with years of love and companionship.*

If you keep more than one guinea pig, be sure to provide enough food for each one.

Feeding

Food

Our first nutritional rule is to feed guinea pigs a source of vitamin C. Guinea pigs, people, and fruit bats are about the only animals that do not make their own vitamin C. Rabbits make their own, dogs do, birds do, but guinea pigs do not. So, they must be fed vitamin C in their diet. Guinea pig pellets have vitamin C added at the factory. That is one thing that makes them different from rabbit pellets. Rabbit pellets also seem a bit richer than guinea pig pellets.

When you buy guinea pig pellets, be sure to buy fresh ones. Vitamin C breaks down in 90 days and is then no longer useful.

If you do feed rabbit pellets during a period when you have run out of guinea pig pellets, just supplement them with vitamin C drops or a natural source of vitamin C. I like to vary (or should I say my guinea pigs like it when I vary) the guinea pigs' dinner. Once in a while I offer rabbit pellets instead of guinea pig pellets. My guinea pigs sometimes go on a "guinea pig pellet strike" and gobble up rabbit pellets instead. This is just because they are spoiled. Most guinea pigs do fine on guinea pig pellets alone.

To obtain fresh vitamin C, guinea pigs enjoy eating orange or grapefruit rinds, tomatoes, and dark green leafy vegetables. Please keep reading! There can be problems with these if fed incorrectly.

An easy way for the owner to feed vitamin C to guinea pigs is for the owner to have fresh-squeezed orange juice or half a grapefruit for breakfast. The guinea pigs can then have the hemisphere-shaped orange or grapefruit rind to eat. Many guinea pigs do not like the tangy fruit itself. When half a grapefruit is placed in with the guinea pigs, they will scurry over to investigate it, stop suddenly, and back up quickly! The sharp fresh citrus smell is a little too much, apparently.

Once they are confident that it is safe, they will plunge their snouts into the circular fruit rind. Their little feet help to steady the rocking, unstable orange and hold it still. They love the white pectin rind, which is actually highest in vitamin C (smart pigs!). Grapefruits may present a problem for smaller guinea pigs, who delight in discovering new places to sit. If the grapefruit is to be eaten and not sat in, cut the rind into two pieces. After eating grapefruit or orange rinds, Peruvian and Silkie guinea pigs need to groom their fronts and long cheek fur because they get sticky juice all

Feeding

Feeding

over their little "ruffs."

Tomatoes are also an excellent source of vitamin C. Some guinea pigs refuse fresh tomatoes but may love V-8 juice, which "looks like tomato juice." I poured some V-8 juice into my guinea pig's plastic dish one day, and she lapped it up! She needed to wash her face and front a bit afterwards, though.

The green leafy vegetables are only a treat! I repeat—a treat and not a main course! They can cause diarrhea in guinea pigs and must *always* be crisp and fresh. Give your pets only greens you would eat. If they are too brown around the edges or too limp to serve as a salad, do not give them to your guinea pigs! Some choice greens are lettuce, kale, romaine, celery greens (not sticks—the stringy parts are hard to digest), and cabbage. Good quality hay is another source of some vitamin C. It also provides the very necessary roughage.

When feeding any pets, it is always a good idea to check two things. One is their water supply. You should know how much water your pet usually drinks in a day. If he or she begins to drink much less (or more), this could indicate a health problem. If your guinea pigs are not eating enough, there may not be enough water. Occasionally

Opposite:
EDIBLE PLANTS: 1. Dock (Rumex crispus); *2. Shepherds Purse* (Capsella bursapastoris); *3. Chickweed* (Stellaria media); *4. Dandelion* (Taraxacum officinale); *5. Vetch* (Vicia sylvatica); *6. Goose grass, cleavers (*Galium aparine); *7. Sow thistle* (Sonchus ateraceus); *8. Groundsel* (Senecia vulgaris); *9. Yarrow, milfoil* (Achillea millafolium); *10. Colts foot* (Tussilago farfara); *11. Goutweed, groundelder* (Aegoxilium podagravia); *12. Avens* (Geum urbanum); *13. Knapweed, hardheads* (Centaurea nigra); *14. Plantain* (Plantaginacea); *15. Tare* (Vicia hirsuta); *16. Bramble* (Rubus saxatilis). *Illustration by Patsy Swanborough.*

Feeding

the little ball in the stem of the water bottle can become caught. The result is no available water. Also, water bottles sometimes drip and leak out the water you have carefully provided. Of course, the other possibility is a negligent or careless owner who has forgotten to check the guinea pigs' water supply. This last occurrence should never happen, but if it does happen once, try going without water or a beverage yourself for a day. That usually is an amazing reminder when you need to provide for the needs of your dependent friends.

The second thing to check is the guinea pigs' droppings. They should be medium-sized and longish, not round. If they are very soft or if the guinea pig has diarrhea, check the diet. Too many greens can quickly cause diarrhea, and this can cause dehydration.

Some guinea pigs confound their owners because they do not eat enough. Most guinea pig owners have just the opposite problem, and we will get to them shortly. For an underweight guinea pig, try providing tasty favorite foods and hay. As mentioned earlier, guinea pigs do need roughage in their diet. Provide fresh, good-quality hay or alfalfa hay cubes for the guinea pigs to chew. Guinea pigs live longer, healthier lives if they have hay.

Opposite:
POISONOUS PLANTS: 1. Mayweed (Anthemis cotula); *2. Common horsetail* (Equisetum arvense); *3. Charlock* (Brassica sinapis); *4. Ragwort* (Senecio jacobaea); *5. Black nightshade* (Solanum nigrum); *6. Deadly nightshade* (Atropa belladonna); *7. Monkshood* (Aconitum napellus); *8. Hemlock* (Conium maculatum); *9. Bracken* (Pteris aquilina); *10. Spurge* (Euphorbia peplus); *11. Privet* (Ligustrum vulgare); *12. Yew* (Taxus baccata); *12. Bastard toadflax* (Thesium humifusum); *13. White bryony* (Bryonia doica); *14. Bindweed* (Convolvulus septum). *Illustration by Patsy Swanborough.*

29

Feeding

Some guinea pigs (I had one) will not eat lettuce or hay. My guinea pig's veterinarian suggested a little guinea pig psychology. "Try cabbage," she said. "It has more taste than the other greens, and we may convince him to eat what is good for him."

If anyone else has this stubborn guinea pig problem, try a little psychology on him. My guinea pig did not know what to do with the cabbage, so I gave some to his rabbit friend. She chewed it up eagerly. The guinea pig listened intently to the crunching, scooted over to the rabbit, and poked his nose up to her mouth to investigate. He sniffed the cabbage on her breath, sniffed the cabbage leaves, and put two and two together. He cautiously tried a nibble, and that launched his career on gourmet cavy food.

Like people, different guinea pigs have different food preferences. My Abyssinian prefers tomatoes but will willingly eat a piece of banana peel if her friend is having one. Like children, guinea pigs will often copy their companions.

Wild grasses that can be used as occasional treats. Left to right: wild barley, meadow brome, barren brome.

Water

Your guinea pig must have fresh water daily. It is best to provide your pet guinea pig with water from a gravity-flow water bottle instead of from a dish. They can easily, and happily, spill a dish and flood their house, kick shavings into the dish during scurrying games of tag, or drop food pellets into the dish when going for a drink. Either way, the water will become messy. They will drink about one and a half to three ounces daily. They drink more in hot, humid weather.

Guinea pigs have an unusual drinking habit. They grab the stem of the bottle in their mouths and begin to tug on it. They may lap the end of the stem to get the water, or they may tug on it until the jerking lets drops of water fall into their mouths.

A plastic bottle with a screw top is preferable to one with a rubber stopper because of the guinea pigs' habit of tugging on the water tube. A good yank can easily unplug a rubber stopper and douse the animal and his home.

Sometimes during the little tugging game they sit back and seem to chew their water. They must be doing something else, perhaps rinsing their mouths or

Feeding

Gravity-feed water bottle in use.

available for small mammals. The type you may want depends on the quality of your local water. If a certain mineral is absent, a spool containing that mineral may be helpful to your pets. Usually salt is unnecessary because it is added to the guinea pig pellets. Also, a salt lick will rust through a wire cage. Don't ruin a cage just to provide an extra treat.

Vitamins may be added to the water. If you are concerned about your pet getting as much vitamin C as he needs, vitamin C drops can be added. Each animal can have about 20 mg of vitamin C per 100 ml of water. Water bottles are measured in milliliters (ml) and are usually 500 ml capacity (1 gallon = 3,800 ml).

Two drops of baby vitamins may be added to the guinea pig pellets if they like the smell of cod-liver oil or whatever odor the vitamins have. You might try giving a drop from an eyedropper right in your guinea pig's mouth. However, be ready for a fight. My always cooperative Peruvian would open her mouth for the vitamins. My always contrary Abyssinian would "squeap" (screaming in guinea pig talk) and push my hands and the dropper away with her front feet. Once I managed to get the eyedropper in the corner of her mouth, she would

thinking about other things, but they appear to be chewing. Then, to top off the procedure, they squirt water back up the tube between drinks, so the inside of the water bottle becomes slimy. This means you have to daily rinse the bottle and scrub it out every week or two.

Snacks

Two additional items *may* be added to your guinea pigs' food list. These are salt and vitamins. Guinea pigs enjoy a salt lick. There are different types of salt spools

Feeding

happily lap on it to get the vitamins. Yet each time we went through the same procedure. She seemed convinced I was trying to poison her even though she loved the vitamins.

The essential vitamins are usually included in the commercial pellets, though you may want to compare the contents lists of different brands. Much of it reads like the contents lists of your breakfast cereal. Guinea pig pellets are a complete feed, so you will find many minerals and vitamins included. The protein percentage will be 16% to 20%. Because of all the added nutrients, guinea pig pellets can be fed by themselves with just hay.

Enclosures intended primarily for use as aquariums and terrariums should be used for guinea pigs purely on a short-term temporary basis and not for permanent housing.

The guinea pigs' snack or supplement list can include tiny pieces of pear or apple, graham crackers, a grape or two, and oats or raw oatmeal. All these little tidbits are practical for a single or two-pet owner. A breeder will keep the feeding as simple as possible. For one thing, it is confusing to try to remember who eats cabbage, who won't touch carrots, etc. The oats or raw oatmeal can be fed by the pet owner or by one who has a colony of guinea pigs. Oats are nutritious, delicious, and (I've been told) apparently help promote hair growth. This can be important to those who have the long-haired Peruvians and Silkies. If they have acquired the habit of hair chewing, the owner wants to know about anything that would help the hair grow more quickly.

Food Dishes

Does it matter whether you use everyday china or the best china for serving your guinea pig his meals? Actually, the china probably will not be the best for him, but the dinnerware will make a difference to you and perhaps to the guinea pig.

Your best bet is a small, weighted plastic bowl. (They don't exactly

Feeding

come in designer colors, but you can get them in primary colors.) Guinea pigs will sit in a large crockery dish. Do not be surprised if your guinea pig learns to tip over his food dish. Some of the smarter guinea pigs (like yours and mine) have learned from other guinea pigs (or visiting rabbits) and pass the

Pet shops sell a variety of cages suitable for guinea pigs.

lessons along. They usually sniff the pellets, reach across the bowl, and up-end it. That scatters the pellets and seems to make a more appealing array since they will then eat the pellets left in the dish.

An alternative feeder is a metal hopper that is usually available for rabbits. It fastens to the outside of the cage and you pour in the correct amount of food. The food drops to the trough section, where the guinea pig eats. Of course you never fill up a hopper or food dish arbitrarily. Measure the correct amount of food. An average adult guinea pig eats about one-third of a cup or two ounces of pellets a day.

The hopper may be difficult to attach to your guinea pig's cage (depending on the type of cage), so most people use the heavy plastic bowls or small food crocks. They must be small enough that the guinea pigs do not sit in them and heavy enough to prevent frequent spilling.

It is important not to overfeed your guinea pig. Obesity can be a strain on the animal's system and is dangerous to a pregnant female. Your pet should feel solid when you hold him, but not fat. He should not have any rolls of fat on the sides. Also, he should be shaped like a brick with the corners cut off, not like a mandolin or blimp.

Housing and Equipment

Now that you can select a healthy looking guinea pig and know what to feed him or her, you can get his house ready. Of course all these things should be done before actually bringing home your new friend. A pet should arrive at a home that is all prepared for him, so he can be comfortable, well fed, and secure right away.

Any animal moving into a new situation will be nervous. The more you can do to ease the transition, the less stress will be on your pet. Try to learn as much as possible about your new friend before you have him move in. People who travel to foreign countries find their stay is more pleasant if they have learned a little of the language, are familiar with the native habits and foods, and know what to expect. You will have a more successful time with your guinea pig if you are familiar with his needs and know what to expect. So, let's get the guinea pig house ready.

The House

I am often asked how much room a guinea pig needs. A guinea pig's house or cage should be as big as you can afford and comfortably accommodate. "The bigger, the better" is a good saying for guinea pig houses. Guinea pigs like to run and need exercise like any other animal. Many people think guinea pigs do not need much space or are boring because they sit in the corner of the 1 foot by 1 foot cage. Of course they do not run around in that cage! There isn't any room!

Regardless of all other considerations, a hutch placed outdoors should be able to be securely latched

The guidelines for sanitation and comfort are the same for guinea pigs as for most other animals. The house must be clean, dry, safe, draft-free, and well ventilated. Before

Housing and Equipment

1. *"Bird cage" style of guinea pig cage, suitable for use in an apartment. 2. Hutch with removable section that can be used for temporary housing on lawn, etc. 3. Hutch equipped with an awning that can be rolled down during inclement weather.*

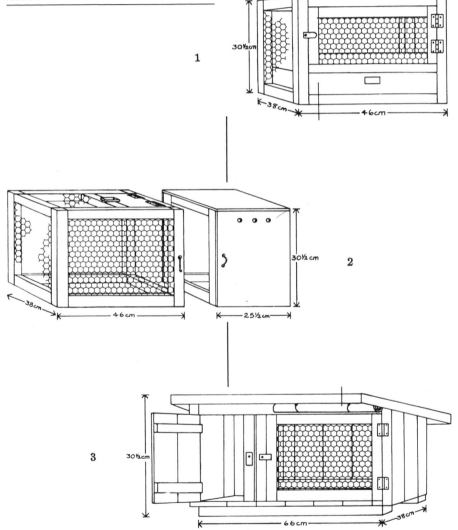

1

2

3

Housing and Equipment

purchasing your guinea pig's home, also keep in mind your comfort and ease for when you clean and maintain the house. Obtain a cage that will be easy for you to clean.

You will not need as complex a home as for a rabbit or as small a one as for the small rodent pets like gerbils or hamsters. Guinea pigs are really medium-sized small mammals. They also have much different habits from their smaller mouse-like cousins.

Free-standing hutch intended for use outdoors. A shutter for use in bad weather is shown to the left of the hutch. Guinea pigs should not be housed in outdoor hutch facilities except for very limited periods of time; even in mild weather, outdoor hutches should be only temporary quarters.

Housing For A Pet

A guinea pig's home should have a solid floor but should not have solid walls. The solid floor is better than a wire floor because wire will make their feet and hocks sore. The soles of a guinea pig's feet are bare, with little pads like the soles of sneakers. The guinea pigs can catch their toes in the wire. A wire floor also allows heat to escape through the bottom of the cage. The walls should not be solid; guinea pigs require ventilation, and solid walls block ventilation.

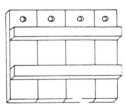

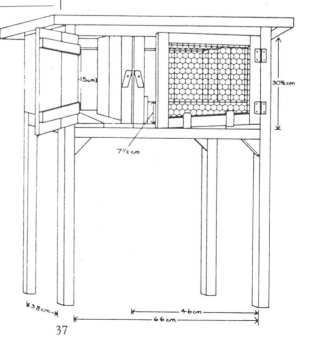

15cm

30½cm

7½cm

38cm

46cm

66cm

Housing and Equipment

Many of the cages sold in pet shops for use with guinea pigs and other small mammals are fine, because they combine solid plastic or metal floors with non-solid walls; the floors are usually of plastic or metal and the sides in the form of metal wires or bars. The floors of such cages often are removable for easy cleaning, which is a distinct advantage.

In general it almost always is better to buy a suitable cage than to try to construct one on your own, but if you are going to try to make one for yourself you'll have to keep in mind the major requirements. As already noted, you'll want to have a solid floor but non-solid walls; you'll also want to make sure that the cage is big enough.

For a one- or two-pet owner, I would recommend a home 2 feet by 4 feet. For the floor you can buy a sheet of tempered Masonite (hardboard). If you know someone who has carpentry skills or can hammer a nail pretty well, build a simple frame into which you can drop the Masonite.

Next buy a roll of hardware cloth. This is really a medium weight wire screen that is perfect for guinea pig-house walls. The wire openings are ¼" or ½" square. The walls need to be only 1 foot high. Tuck the hardware cloth under the Masonite floor or staple it right to the inside of the frame. Bingo. Your house is done.

You will soon find that a 3-inch border around the walls will help keep everything neat. The border can be tiny screen or Plexiglas. This little guard wall will keep the shavings in the guinea pig's cage instead of around the cage, across the room, and in everything else.

Guinea pigs usually select one corner of their cage as the main bathroom. This corner can be picked out daily and even scrubbed with a mild soap once every week or two.

The tempered Masonite is conditioned on one side to be water resistant. Put that side up for the cage floor because it will last longer than the absorbent side. The tempered side is easy to recognize. It is shiny and slippery and is the side your pet will skid on when it is new.

When you see that the tempered surface is worn through in the frequented corners or is beginning to have an odor, just remove it and replace it with a new floor.

Some of you are anxious to hear what happened to the ceiling or cage lid to secure the little beasts. Do not worry, and kids, please let your parents know this. Guinea pigs are not escape artists like their mouse, gerbil, and, especially, hamster cousins. Guinea pigs do not climb

Housing and Equipment

up screen walls and rarely attempt escape. The cage walls should be high enough to provide the illusion of confinement, however.

If there are any cats, dogs, or young children in the house, however, you will want to construct a roof to *protect* your guinea pig. Put your guinea pig house up on a table or some secure stand about 3 feet high. This is an easier height for you to clean at and will keep the guinea pig out of floor drafts. It also keeps it away from other investigating pets that could by accident gain access to the room. Do not imagine that your sweet kitty or Fido would never harm your little friend—don't tempt them.

If a house as large as I described is not practical for you, then be assured there are other good homes. The cage should be at least 2 feet by 2 feet and can have a solid wooden floor or a removable metal tray. Both are easy to clean.

Pens are a good alternative, especially for breeders of guinea pigs. These are usually about 2 feet by 2 feet and 15 inches high, which provides adequate ventilation. For a guinea pig colony, tiered pens are made. Tiers are arranged in steps, or the pens are set directly above each other.

The floors of these pens can be made of wood, but stainless steel or fiberglass would be easier to clean. Most guinea pig colony pens are constructed of sturdy, heavy gauge wire. The doors open inward and latch onto the wire ceiling. That way the door is up out of the way when the owner needs to feed, pet, or remove the resident. The pens may have removable partitions of wood, aluminum, or mesh (hardware cloth) on frames.

If a caviary, or place with many guinea pigs, is in a garage or basement, no pesticide strips should be around. The fumes from the chemicals can make the guinea pigs sick.

You might want to visit several guinea pig breeders to view their pens to judge which would best suit you, your space, and needs.

Never house a guinea pig in a fishtank or aquarium. Aquaria may be ideal homes for gerbils, but they are *not* for guinea pigs. An aquarium is far too small for an active guinea pig. Most importantly, guinea pigs need fresh air ventilation. Warm, stale air will sit in a fishtank. Guinea pigs cannot withstand heat and humidity, and a closed four-sided glass aquarium will become humid. The guinea pig will not have fresh dry air to breathe and will become sick. Some guinea pig breeders even

Housing and Equipment

air-condition their caviary to provide fresh air for their animals.

An aquarium must never be set in a window, by the way. It can heat up and cause heat prostration in any pet.

A Cavy In Your Room?

People can be extremely allergic to guinea pigs, so anyone who has an allergy or asthma should be very careful around guinea pigs. Children especially may insist on keeping their pet guinea pig in their closed room, which will become warm and dry. The guinea pig's loose hair and dry skin (from low humidity) can make an allergy worse or at least irritate the lungs.

Bedding

What type of bedding is best? Bedding is of utmost importance for keeping the guinea pigs' home dry and clean.

SHAVINGS

Laboratory or kiln-dried shavings are your first choice because they are dust-free, fluffy, and absorbent. They are often available from grain mills or feed stores in large bags for a very reasonable amount. One of these

bags will last two guinea pigs several months. Spread any shavings about 1 inch deep over the cage floor.

Dust-free shavings are advantageous to both the guinea pigs' and the owner's respiratory systems. Guinea pigs are susceptible to respiratory ailments, so these shavings are best for that reason, too.

Cedar shavings are easy to obtain, although they usually are also expensive. They make good bedding but will sometimes turn the guinea pig's belly red. This would be a definite disadvantage if you have a white guinea pig or plan to show your pet in a cavy show.

PEANUT SHELLS

These are supposed to be great bedding, too. In some areas horses are bedded with peanut shells. They are light, absorbent, and can be provided by the owner if you are a real peanut fanatic!

HAY OR STRAW

These can become wet and soiled fairly easily. Also, the guinea pigs like to nibble on the hay, which they should not do if it is soiled.

POOR BEDDINGS

Do not use sawdust or newspaper for your guinea pigs. Sawdust mats and gets wet easily. It can irritate the lungs of your pal, too.

Newspaper is absorbent, but guinea pigs love to chew it. Their rodent teeth grow continuously and need to be worn down. That is why they like to chew. Unlike gerbils who will shred newspaper for a bed, guinea pigs will just eat it. That is not good for them— the lead in the newsprint ink can make them sick.

The Nest

Guinea pigs love to nestle into corners. They love to sit on or under things too. You can provide a snug nestbox made of wood. It must be very steady. A plywood box will be a good house. It will provide a cozy hideaway and a roof upon which to climb. It must be made of plain wood. Your guinea pigs will chew at the box edges, so you do not want them to eat any paint.

Forget about using a shoebox. It is a perfect size for the guinea pig to sit in, crawl through, or crawl upon. However, because it is cardboard it will soon disappear. Your pigs will love to eat it up.

A shoebox-size house is ideal, however. Make sure there is very easy access and exit space. Maybe have it three-sided. Tilt the box onto one long side, so one side is the floor. Then one whole side is open. If a guinea pig gets caught in a box when trying to turn around, it will panic.

Guinea pigs enjoy climbing little ramps, sitting on provided shelves, and sitting under things. I learned that a lean-to made of a thin board leaning against the top of the walls provided a cozy sleeping place for my guinea pigs. But when I acquired my young Abyssinian, she quickly scurried up the lean-to and out over the edge of the cage. (She was caught in mid-air.) So although guinea pigs do not climb up walls like mice, they may traipse up an easier incline and get into trouble. Be sure you check for potential steps to escape. Stay with your pets when you introduce a new box or shelf to be sure they will not get into trouble.

Housekeeping

Remember, whether you have one pet or 20 show-quality guinea pigs, they all deserve to be well cared for and kept in a roomy, comfortable, clean home. Cleanliness is vital for your pet's health and a pleasant home.

Also remember that a caged guinea pig depends on his owner for all his

Housing and Equipment

needs. A caged pet really relies on you. You must make his needs part of your daily routine and habits. Simply picking out the soiled corner of his cage each day at the same time makes caring for your guinea pig easy. Then once every week or two he can get an entire new set of shavings. His floor can get a quick scrub with a mild disinfectant, too. Remember to rinse the cage after disinfecting, and be sure it is dry before replacing your pet.

During housecleaning the guinea pig can be set happily in a cardboard box or a little roofless pen. If your room is safe, the guinea pig can also have "rec" (recreation) time while investigating your room.

Free-roaming Pigs?

"Rec" time can easily turn into "wreck" time if you are not careful. Your guinea pig will love it, but there are dangers to him in your house.

If a guinea pig is going to be allowed to roam loose in a room, the room must be "guinea pig proofed." First block off any crawl spaces under a couch, bureau, or behind a refrigerator or stove.

Secondly, secure all wires and electric cords out of the path and reach of the guinea pig. Guinea pigs are not as aggressive with cords as rabbits are, but guinea pigs will nibble on wires lying on the floor in front of them.

Step three is to pick up your clothes! A sweater, T-shirt, or pants make a terrific nest for a guinea pig. That in itself might not be a problem, but when guinea pigs make nests they usually go to the bathroom there. They also nibble on their surroundings. You can recognize a guinea pig owner by the peculiar little holes in his shirts and pantlegs. You may not mind (since it is a conversation piece), but be forewarned.

Obviously the other factor about loose guinea pigs is that they cannot be housebroken. Some very smart guinea pigs will use a newspaper a high percentage of the time, but you cannot depend on that.

The last important precaution in guinea pig proofing a room is to make absolutely sure that the door is never left open to allow an escape or to allow a pet dog or cat to enter. Chances are that a dog or cat will try to chase the guinea pig. Even if they are only curious, they can really frighten the guinea pig, which is timid by nature.

As you can see, there are numerous ways that guinea pigs can be housed successfully. One last

Handling

point should be made though. Guinea pigs are quieter if each is housed in his own space. (It sounds like an encounter group idea, but it is true.) The guinea pig does not have to compete at all for the water bottle, the food, or a sleeping place. As a matter of fact, the guinea pig will probably select one corner to sleep in all the time. Guinea pigs who are housed in groups are wilder. They may actually need to be wilder to get what they want and to keep from being bothered by their companions.

If it works out easily for the caretaker (you), it is nice to house guinea pigs in suitable pairs. This may be too difficult to determine if there are a lot of animals, but where a few are involved it might be feasible. With congenial pairs you will see a lot of interesting behavior. The dominant one will get the water bottle first, for example. Dominance is determined by the water, not the food. Dominance is unrelated to weight. Also, each guinea pig will have a favorite corner to sit in. They can become more dependent on their companion than you realize. When one of the guinea pigs dies, the survivor may adopt the other's corner for sleeping. It almost seems a kind of comfort for the survivor.

Much of the fun of having a pet is being able to hold him, pet him, and carry him around with you. There are ways of doing this that will make it enjoyable for both of you.

First of all, guinea pigs love to be petted. However, for handling to be enjoyable for the guinea pig, the handler must be sure he does not frighten or injure the guinea pig.

For a novice, picking up a guinea pig can be an unnerving experience, especially if this novice thinks of guinea pigs as rats without tails (and this person is afraid of rats). Guinea pigs have an interesting habit when you reach in to pick them up. They run, they race, they stop and start quickly. If a nervous person is trying to pick up the racing rodent, he may be anxious and also scare the guinea pig by plunging or lunging at him.

When a guinea pig takes off for this game of tag, quietly edge him into a corner and place your hand over his shoulders. Usually the guinea pig will crouch when you do this. Then slide your hand under the hindquarters and scoop him up securely with both hands.

Always use two hands when you hold a guinea pig. You have two, use them both. Also always move slowly and quietly around guinea pigs. They become startled easily. This probably

Handling

is due to their ancient history in South America. Their ancestors were nocturnal prey (or dinners) for other animals! They had to be alert and quick to survive. Our domestic guinea pigs also are alert and quick. A sudden noise or movement sends them dashing for protection.

You will find that your guinea pig prefers two positions when he is being held. One position is sitting on your hand and forearm while you gently hold him next to you. He feels safe when he is held this way. He is sitting almost on a shelf and has you to lean against, too.

The second position that a guinea pig likes is to be held facing upward. He will sit on your holding hand and crawl up your chest, so that he is almost standing. Your responsibility is to place your hand over his back so that he feels secure.

The important thing to remember is to make your guinea pig feel secure and safe. Do not leave his feet hanging out somewhere. Use both hands gently and hold his whole body. Do not pick him up by the shoulders, front legs, or belly. Put one hand under the front end and one hand under the hind end.

There is one guinea pig characteristic you need to know about. They are the "fastest backers in the West." They back up very

quickly and with little warning. So always have one hand a little behind the hindquarters in case your pet throws himself into reverse.

When your guinea pig stands up (crawls up toward your chin when you are holding him), realize that he may try to hop up higher, especially if he trusts you and is nervous about a situation. For an example, let us take everyone's favorite place: the doctor's. When the veterinarian is examining your chum, your guinea pig may scurry to you, put his front feet up on your shirt, and try to jump up into your arms. Once up there he may try for the shoulder or neck.

Another interesting guinea pig peculiarity is that they seem to prefer facing in one direction when they are held. Maybe the owner usually carries them facing to the right because he is right handed. He will always pick up the guinea pig the same way. Try this with your guinea pig. If you usually have him facing to the right, try to turn him around so that he is facing to the left. Many guinea pigs will twist back around or face upward rather than face the new direction.

We have discussed how to be careful with your little friend. There is one more thing you should be aware of. Remember that guinea pigs cannot be house broken? Be forewarned then. They sometimes have accidents when they are sitting on you. Therefore you may want to hold them on a folded towel so you do not get wet. I have found that my guinea pigs start to talk a little more and make their little noises louder as a warning beforehand. Actually they only do that sometimes, so I am often taken by surprise, too.

Guinea Pig Noises

You are going to hear guinea pig noises when you are handling your guinea pig, so I think you might like a translation of their various sounds.

Guinea pigs are the most vocal of the small mammals. Their most identifiable and well-known noise is the high-pitched whistle or "wheep." They open their mouths widely and pull their ears back when they whistle. In guinea pig talk it means "Give me some food!" They will say this when they hear you near the refrigerator or when you rustle a plastic bag. (Bags usually hold lettuce.) They will "wheep" when you have been in the kitchen long enough in the morning and have not yet brought breakfast to them. They will whistle when you whistle to them.

When you do whistle, remember you are saying "Food!" to them, so do not tease them by whistling and not giving them their treat. You may want to show your friends how smart and cute your guinea pigs are by whistling to them. They, of course, will whistle back and usually run up to the edge of the cage and look expectantly at you. At least they will run around in circles whistling.

Sound number two is very much like the "wheep" whistle. This second whistle is slower and does not have the excited sound and repetition of the "Dinner, please" whistle. Guinea pigs use this when frightened and possibly when protesting. If you corner your guinea pig and try to pick him up or slide him out from under a bureau or whatever he is under, he will open his mouth widely and let out this scream-like "wheeeeep!". Some guinea pigs do it at the veterinarian's, too. They may scream when the veterinarian is palpating their inner organs or when their nails are being clipped. It is rather embarrassing for the veterinarian, who is trying to be very gentle while his patient is screaming for help. Maybe someone can tell me if Abyssinians seem to do this more than other guinea pigs. My Abyssinians, especially as youngsters, always screamed at the veterinarian.

Sound number three is the purr.

Handling

Boy guinea pigs purr at girl guinea pigs, and girls do it at girl guinea pigs, too. It is a sexual courtship sound and precedes mating. It is accompanied by a slow swaying from side to side. Sometimes a female in heat will mount another female and make this sound beforehand.

I have seen one guinea pig purring and slowly advancing toward another guinea pig like "the blob" inching forward. The other guinea pig chattered her teeth nervously and began to make tiny peeps which definitely seemed to be cries of concern. Finally the pursued victim escaped on top of the little shoebox-size house. The aggressor swayed over, actually stood up on her hind feet with her front feet on the box, and purred loudly. So the purring is a mating sound and possibly a sound of dominance also.

Sound number four is the aforementioned teeth chattering. Guinea pigs grind their teeth back and forth when they are nervous and anxious.

Sound number five is the anxious little peep. This is not as common a sound as the others. At least it is rare among trusting, happy guinea pigs.

Sound number six is the purring shudder. A loud noise or jingle will alarm a guinea pig. Their reaction is to give a two-second "Brrrr." It is

rather like someone who has suddenly taken a chill. Obviously you try to minimize the sounds that upset your guinea pig. They also make this noise if you pet their hips and tickle them.

Sound number seven is the burbling little bird-like noise. This is fairly soft and indicates contentment. A guinea pig who is being held by his or her favorite person will often make this sound as he is being stroked.

Sound number eight is the chutt-chutt-chutt. Guinea pigs are famous for this sound. A similar sound is combined with the aforementioned burble when they are happy to be petted. This chutt-chutt-chutt is also the exploring sound. Guinea pigs investigate new surroundings in a careful manner. They move forward in a series of stops and starts like rush-hour traffic. The nose is usually poked out in front and held fairly high or bobbed up and down. Little chutt-chutt-chutt noises are made at the same time.

Sound number nine ties in with the contented burble, too. It is almost a whine. Parents often are alarmed when they hear it. They are afraid the guinea pig is being hurt while held. This sound is pretty easy to imitate in case you want to start an avocation of guinea pig

Handling

calls. (Many people can do bird calls, but how many do you hear doing guinea pig calls?)

There are other noises and tones that guinea pigs make. Someone has identified 30 distinct sounds! They are hard to describe, of course, but a careful study of all the vocalizations could give hours of interesting work.

Every One Is Different

You will notice that many guinea pigs do not like to have their chin or feet touched. The Abyssinians I have known do not want to be stroked under the chin. Their response is to immediately set one of their front feet on your fingers. Other breeds may like chin stroking quite a bit. Peruvians may love to have their long fur gently pulled under their chin. They will lift their chin and stretch much like a cat who loves being petted in one special place. Guinea pigs who do not like having their feet touched make it tricky business to clip their nails.

Guinea pigs have an appealing head lifting gesture. They will do this when they are being held and petted across the head. Suddenly they will thrust the nose up as if pushing away your hand. This is really quite cute if you need to

convince a friend or a parent that this little rodent is really harmless.

Every guinea pig may display these behaviors. Every guinea pig also seems to think up a few peculiar traits of his own. Whether it is displayed in behavior, noises, eating preferences, or whatever, each guinea pig is definitely an individual.

Many times people give guinea pigs as gifts to children or guinea pigs are kept as classroom pets. They are easy for children to handle and will be gentle if handled properly. If a teacher is going to adopt a guinea pig to have as a classroom pet, he or she must check with all the children concerning allergies. Children who have allergies may be terribly allergic to guinea pigs.

Abyssinian guinea pig.

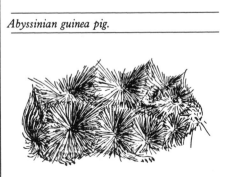

Health Care

A happy guinea pig is a healthy guinea pig, or vice versa. The guinea pig that you select should be healthy, properly fed, and properly housed if you have followed my previous suggestions. Remember that your guinea pig or guinea pigs are living things who depend on you. They depend on you for food, water, shelter, exercise, veterinary care, and love. They cannot take care of their own needs, so they really rely on you. You can help your guinea pig stay healthy and enjoy a happy lifetime by being aware of potential problems and practicing preventive medicine.

Signs of a Healthy Animal

First let us acquaint ourselves with the signs of a healthy animal. A healthy animal has clear, bright eyes, a nice clean nose, and clean ears. A healthy animal also has a smooth, shiny coat. The animal will be active and alert.

To ensure that he remains healthy, every pet should visit the veterinarian for an annual check-up. A guinea pig's physical examination is very much like our own examination at the doctor's. The doctor (or veterinarian) checks the eyes, ears, nose, breathing, heart, abdomen, lymph glands, and vital statistics.

You can do a simple "vet check" at home for your own pet guinea pig. You might even want to maintain a chart to record your guinea pig's health and statistics.

The Vet Check

The vital statistics that a veterinarian would gather are sex, weight, age, pulse, respiration, and temperature of your guinea pig.

A guinea pig's sex is pretty easy to determine. Pick up the guinea pig with both hands (you remember how important that is) and gently tilt your pet to a sitting up position. Then you can see the genital area easily. If the opening is shaped like a Y, it is a female. If it is shaped like an X, it is a male.

A guinea pig can be weighed on a baby scale. The guinea pig usually will sit on it when placed there. When the scale stops jiggling it can be read. The average weight of an adult is two pounds. Females generally weigh less than males. A baby guinea pig usually weighs roughly three ounces. Its birth weight will depend on the number of babies born in the litter and on the health of the mother. At weaning time (21 days) a young guinea pig will weigh about eight and a half ounces.

Health Care

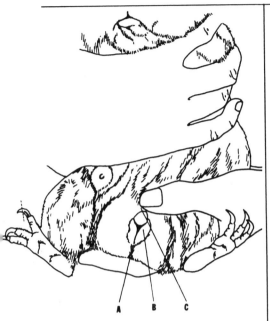

The age of the guinea pig is something the owner has to know, since there is no reliable method of determining a guinea pig's age. The teeth of a horse can be checked for wear and their age can be determined that way. But most other domestic animals do not have an easy way to check on age. A guinea pig's average life span is five years. They can live for seven years or longer, although it is unusual.

The normal pulse or heart beat of a guinea pig is 240-280/minute. You can check the pulse yourself. Use a watch with a second hand and count

Above: Genital area of male guinea pig. A = anus; B = scrotal sac area; C = point at which slight pressure can be applied to make penis protrude.

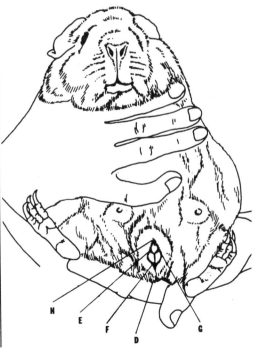

Right: Genital area of female guinea pig. D = anus; E, F and G = hairless areas; H = urethral opening.

the pulse for 15 seconds. You will be able to actually feel the heart beat by placing your fingers on the chest just behind the guinea pig's elbow. Multiply the number of beats in 15 seconds by four and you have the pulse rate per minute.

The normal respiration rate of guinea pigs is 60-90/minute. That is harder to measure and perhaps not as vital. If you want to figure out the respiration rate, try watching the guinea pig's flanks. The flank is the area just in front of the hip bone. You can see the flank move up and down with each breath.

A guinea pig's normal temperature is 102.2° to 104° Fahrenheit or 39° to 40° Celsius. A guinea pig's normal temperature can vary two or three degrees from that of other guinea pigs. It is important to know your own animal's temperature.

A guinea pig's nails must be trimmed regularly. The veterinarian can do this and so can the owner. Use regular fingernail clippers. The guinea pig probably will not enjoy this, but it should not hurt them if you are careful. However, guinea pigs tend to become anxious when their nails are done. Be careful to hold each foot gently and do not squeeze. If your guinea pig has white or lightly colored nails, you will be able to clearly see the quick

or blood vessel. You want to cut only the extra nail and not the quick. If you do cut to the quick, your guinea pig will scream once (at least) and his nail will bleed. Tell him you are sorry and pat cornstarch onto the nail. It will stop the bleeding. Then be more careful.

On the underside of the nail a groove begins beyond the quick. If the nail is black this groove may help you to avoid the quick.

You can spot a basically healthy guinea pig now. The remainder of this chapter deals with potential problems and some preventive medicine.

Eyes

The eyes should be clear and bright. Any discharge from the eyes, whether clear, white, or yellowish, should be regarded with suspicion. Occasionally a guinea pig will develop a chronic eye problem. A milky substance may be in the eye and be running from the corner. A veterinarian should check to determine whether the infection is restricted to the eye alone. It could be associated with a cold or an irritation of the respiratory system. If it is strictly an eye infection, an ointment like Panalog applied three times a day should clear it up in a few days.

If the surface of the eye has a light blue mark, it could be a scar due to an injury. Some hay might have poked your guinea pig in the eye. The veterinarian can inform you as to whether it is just a scar or if it is an ulcer. The veterinarian will put eyedrops in the eye to see if it takes a stain. Your guinea pig will probably scream protests, but it does not hurt. If the eye does take stain, that means there may be an ulcer problem. Your veterinarian will recommend action depending on the findings.

A light blue, glassy look is probably the beginning of a cataract. It will seem to reflect the light. This condition is not common but may develop in older animals. It is probably not common because many guinea pigs do not live to be six, seven, or eight years old. Those cataracts that develop with old age are called senile cataracts. If your older guinea pig does have difficulty seeing, you can help him by letting him know when you are there. Be sure to talk to him and get his attention, so he is not startled if his vision is poor and he does not see you. You may have to whistle and speak loudly if your older guinea pig is getting hard of hearing, too.

An unusual bulging of the eyeball can indicate a problem. It should be checked by a veterinarian, especially if the animal has trouble blinking and is acting uncomfortable. This could indicate a really serious problem.

Now please be very familiar with your guinea pig before rushing him to the veterinarian. Notice that if you have a staring contest with your guinea pig, he will always win. Guinea pigs do not blink very often, and their eyeballs are quite round and therefore normally seem to protrude. You may also see the whites of their eyes, particularly on the underside of the iris. Do not worry if that is normal for your particular guinea pig.

Guinea pigs sometimes develop what is called "pea eye." It is an abnormal swelling on the inside eyelid. This is not really serious, but keep an eye on the eyes to be aware of any infection or abnormality. Pea eye will disqualify a guinea pig in a show.

Older guinea pigs may show more white around their eyes. As the muscles and supportive tissue lose their tone, the inner edges of the eyelid will droop. This is normal.

Ears, Nose, and Throat

Let's move on to the ears. A guinea pig's droopy little ears are

Health Care

almost completely hairless on the top. Even with the long-haired Peruvians and Silkies, the ears are easy to see and examine. Every four to six weeks you can carefully clean your guinea pig's ears. A dark, waxy substance can be gently wiped off with some cotton, a plain cotton swab, or a tissue dabbed with mineral oil. Just do the outer ear, being very careful of the little folds and bumps on the inside of the ear and earflap. Do not let any mineral oil drip down into the ear. There should be just enough on the cotton swab to moisten the cotton. This makes it easier to wipe out the ear.

If your guinea pig is shaking his ears a lot or seems to be in discomfort when you gently wipe out the ear, then have a veterinarian check him. Wax build-up or an abscess could be causing discomfort. Only a veterinarian should investigate the inside of the ear. It is too risky for most pet owners to even try to clean that part of the ear.

Around the ear is the area where lice will be seen if your guinea pig ever has them. They are long, thin, and light colored. The eggs can be seen on dark hair.

Check your guinea pig's throat and chin. Everyday when you handle your pet you should do a "once-over." This way you will detect any changes in your guinea pig's condition. I am assuming you handle your guinea pig daily. Every pet, especially the small mammals, should be petted and checked daily. These animals, including guinea pigs, can develop problems quickly. If your pet does become ill, take him to the veterinarian immediately. Some diseases can cause death in 24 to 48 hours. Guinea pigs are sturdier than the smaller rodent pets, like gerbils and hamsters, but they still should receive generous attention.

Why check the chin? Guinea pigs sometimes do get abscesses near the throat. Most of the time they are near or involve the lymph glands under the chin. A veterinarian will carefully lance an abscess and let it drain. Of course, the owner must be sure the wound does not become soiled or infected. The veterinarian will probably prescribe an ointment to put on the area. If it begins oozing a lot or developing heat in the area, it could mean an infection.

Abscesses in guinea pigs seem to be of two kinds. One is a "strep" infection under the neck. It seems to be stress related. Stress can result when a guinea pig is in a new setting, traveling, or experiencing temperature changes or changes in its environment. Be particularly aware under these conditions. A streptococcus infection is also likely if the guinea pig has a respiratory infection.

You can let the abscess develop (it will be rock hard) and then lance it if you are experienced in these things. Otherwise, take a trip to the veterinarian. Warm compresses may help to open the abscess and drain it. Do not let any of the draining matter run onto the bedding. The infection is spread in this way. Use phenol or sulfonamide ointment in the wound.

The second kind of abscess is of toothpaste consistency. It is caused by food caught in the little pockets or indentations in the cheeks. Rabbits can get these too. They can be treated in the same way as any other abscess.

The Coat

A guinea pig's coat should be full and shiny. The different breeds have different kinds of hair, but the coat should be uniform and healthy looking. Vitamin E added to the food can help improve the coat's condition and clear up dander (pet dandruff). Ask the veterinarian how much should be added.

HAIR LOSS

Guinea pigs shed all year, and sometimes it seems they shed when they are nervous. Check your shirt after you and your guinea pig have been to the veterinarian's! They also shed in the spring and fall when they renew their coats.

Unusual hair loss, however, can be an indication of an internal problem. A common cause of hair loss is scurvy or lack of vitamin C. Guinea pigs are one of the few animals that do not make their own vitamin C. Therefore, they need a source of vitamin C from foods like citrus fruits (grapefruits and oranges) and greens. Also, guinea pig pellets have vitamin C added, and vitamin drops added to the water can help prevent scurvy, too.

Remember that vitamin C breaks down quickly. *Fresh* guinea pig pellets are a must to provide vitamin C. If the pellets are older than two months, the efficiency of the vitamin C is questionable.

BARBERING

This obviously is a cause of hair loss, too, although barbering is not usually a nutritional problem like the aforementioned scurvy. Guinea pigs may barber themselves or their companions. This hair chewing can be due to several causes. It is a

Health Care

disaster for Peruvian and Silkie show guinea pigs, since these guinea pigs are judged about 70% on their coat!

Barbering is a chewing habit caused by boredom, excitement, hereditary tendencies, instruction, or even dietary deficiencies. If the cause is boredom it is easy to remedy: Spend more time with your pet, acquire a guinea pig companion, or improve the cage.

Excitement or anxiety may or may not be avoidable. If guinea pigs have to spend a weekend or vacation time with a stranger in a new house, they will be nervous. Through gentle handling and a relatively quiet environment, the guinea pigs will settle down and relax after several days. However, by then a Peruvian may have short bangs or a Mohawk haircut with shorn sides to match.

It seems some guinea pigs have a natural tendency to chew hair. You know the saying "Like father, like son." Barbering apparently could be a family trait. No one knows whether barbering is a hereditary trait. We do know, however, that guinea pigs learn almost everything, if not everything, they do. If a mother guinea pig chews hair, the babies will learn to chew, too.

Guinea pigs may chew their hair due to lack of roughage or the absence of some nutrient. Providing hay for the guinea pig to nibble on can remedy things. Of course, like any behavior, barbering can become a habit. If hay, a peaceful setting, and lots of attention from you do not help to stop the hair chewing, you can always enjoy the new coiffure!

Teeth Problems

Guinea pigs' teeth grow constantly. They need to wear them down by chewing on pellets or hay or something wooden. Occasionally a guinea pig's teeth will overgrow and make eating very difficult. This overgrowth is called malocclusion. The lower front teeth may grow too long and have a great overlap, or the molars will grow unevenly in back. A veterinarian can help the problem by occasionally nipping off the overgrowth. This problem may be hereditary, so you may not want to breed guinea pigs that have malocclusion.

When a guinea pig does have a problem eating, it is more often due to a common ailment rather than malocclusion. Owners and veterinarians often jump to the conclusion that the guinea pig's teeth are overgrown. Look for the obvious common problem first. Look for what you might find in a dog or cat. A guinea pig can bite its

Health Care

cheek, and sometimes that is sore. An abscess or toothache may be the cause, too.

The guinea pig with a mouth problem will act like it is trying to get something out of its mouth or off the back of its tongue. It will open its mouth, paw at the mouth, and put its ears back. It may have bitten its tongue or cheek. If it is sore for a while, the guinea pig may have trouble eating hard foods like carrots. Try keeping the guinea pig on a softer diet like pellets, oats, raw oatmeal, and greens.

Parasites

Parasites are animals (usually insects) which live in or on other animals. The guinea pig can get guinea pig lice and guinea pig mites. They are species-specific, which means they live only on one species, which in this case is the guinea pig. People do not catch lice from their guinea pigs. The lice have special legs that are adapted for holding onto a specific type of hair, so guinea pig lice cannot hold onto human hair. Many parents have worried that their child will catch lice from a classroom pet; rest assured that they will not.

You can actually see lice or mites on a guinea pig. Frequent scratching by the guinea pig also may indicate their presence. Lice settle around the ears and top of the guinea pig's head. They are long, light colored, and can be seen moving. The eggs are round globules that will also be around the ears.

To get rid of lice use an approved powder that would be used for fleas on kittens. Carbaryl (3 to 5%) is the safest insecticide to use. Other flea powders will be too strong for a guinea pig. Always protect the guinea pig's eyes when using this kind of medication. You can spray or dust some of the medicine on a cotton swab to apply it (very carefully) around the area of the eyes.

The lice will actually fall off the guinea pig. Therefore at the same time the animal is being treated, clean the cage or pen thoroughly. Dust on top of the shavings with the same kitten flea powder. If you dust on the floor of the cage, any remaining lice will climb on top of the shavings and then back onto the guinea pig. You can always dust the house after throwing away the soiled shavings.

Mites can be treated in the same way as lice. Mites look like dust on the hair shafts on the rear of the animal. It seems that you normally may see white mites on dark guinea pigs, and dark mites on light guinea pigs. This would help in detection if it were so. You can carefully dip the

Health Care

guinea pig in a lime-sulphur dip usually available for cats or kittens.

Guinea pigs can also get ear mites. You will see persistent scratching. Medicine is available for ear mites at the veterinarian.

Illnesses

The rest of this section on diseases and problems will be only extra knowledge for most of you. Your guinea pig is most likely to remain healthy as long as you are careful with its diet and housing. Most of the following ailments are never seen by those owners who are conscientious and careful with their pet guinea pigs. Do not become a hypochondriac about your pet. He or she will probably remain well. However, you may want to make yourself familiar with certain symptoms of illnesses just so you can know if your friend ever does have a problem.

COCCIDIOSIS

This disease is caused by a protozoan parasite that lives in the intestines. It is not common and is fairly easy to combat. The signs of coccidiosis are diarrhea, loss of appetite, and listlessness.

Below: A trio of star-studded guinea pigs with their winnings.

Two female guinea pigs, one a Cream and the other a Buff.

Above: A covy of Agouti or wild-colored cavies. ***Opposite top:*** A best-in-show-winning (at Greater London Show) Golden Satin guinea pig. ***Opposite below:*** A pregnant pet quality guinea pig.

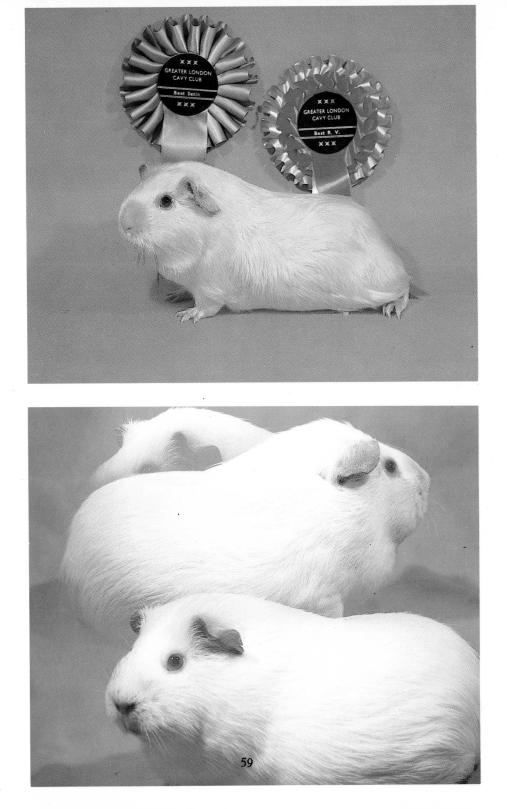

Above: *Some guinea pig varieties are bred for the symmetry of their markings.* ***Opposite:*** *A well-groomed guinea pig is a happier, healthier pet than one that is never brushed.*

Above: Guinea pigs come in a wide variety of colors; there is something for everyone in the cavy spectrum. *Opposite:* A healthy guinea pig will have a clean coat, bright eyes, and an active, inquisitive interest in its surroundings.

Profile of a handsome Abyssinian guinea pig.

Health Care

The disease is passed through the fecal matter or droppings of the guinea pigs. Sanitary conditions can arrest and prevent the spread of coccidiosis. Regular cleaning, especially when the disease is present, will protect your guinea pigs. Guinea pigs, like most animals, lick their feet when grooming. This is an easy way for the eggs of *Eimeria caviae* (the protozoan that causes the disease) to be recycled into the cavy or guinea pig. Fastidious cleaning, therefore, will rid your guinea pigs of the protozoa. Medicine from your veterinarian can be added to the drinking water to control the infection.

DIARRHEA

This is perhaps the most common ailment. Diarrhea can be a serious health hazard to your animals because they can become dehydrated. It is usually caused by feeding too much green food or spoiled food. Remember to feed your pet only greens that you would eat. Never feed greens that are wilted, brown, or unwashed. Withholding all green foods for a few days usually remedies the diarrhea.

FUNGI OR RINGWORM

Guinea pigs and rabbits are more susceptible to ringworm than are other pets. Ringworm is a mycotic, or fungal, infection of the skin. There are two kinds of fungi that affect guinea pigs. They both cause small dark spots around the eyes and other parts of the body. The fungus may be transmitted to people. Ringworm can be treated successfully with griseofulvin fed in the daily diet. This can be obtained from the veterinarian.

METASTATIC CALCIFICATION

It's not as confusing as it sounds. This is a fancy title for a serious problem that can be prevented. Calcium deposits occur in the guinea pig's internal organs (heart, lungs, kidneys, etc.), joints, and muscles. It is most often seen in adult males. The guinea pig loses weight, has stiff joints, and usually dies. The condition is caused by an imbalance of magnesium, calcium, and phosphorus in the guinea pig. It is aggravated by too much vitamin D.

This is a typical example of why a balanced diet is so important. A pet owner or breeder must be sure the animal's diet is properly balanced. It is best to feed commercial foods (guinea pig pellets) to your pets. These foods have been carefully developed to ensure the proper balance of vitamins and minerals for your guinea pig.

Health Care

MUSCULAR DYSTROPHY

Do not worry. This is not common, and it is preventable. Its signs are lameness, stiffness, and a refusal to move. It is due to vitamin E deficiency. Guinea pigs are very sensitive to low vitamin E amounts. Here again, we can stress the importance of proper diet. You can see it is best to feed a commercial food and not rely on table or salad scraps to supply all your guinea pig's needs.

PNEUMONIA

Pneumonia is caused by one of five bacteria or viruses. It is recognized by coughing, sneezing, and/or a discharge from both the eyes and nose. Respiratory ailments all have these symptoms. Pneumonia may be one of the main causes of death in guinea pigs.

Well-ventilated, dry, and draft-free cages help prevent respiratory problems. When they do occur, the irritating environmental problem must first be changed. The guinea pig must be in healthy surroundings. Second, tetracycline can be added to the drinking water (10 mg per 500 grams, or 17½ ounces, of body weight). Third, a vaporizer does help. Do what you would do yourself for a cold. That includes a vaporizer and a

mentholated ointment on the chest. A guinea pig cannot lick its chest near the throat, so it is a safe place to apply the salve.

By the way, guinea pigs are most susceptible to infections from February to May and September to October.

POISONING BY ANTIBIOTICS

Guinea pigs are very susceptible to the toxic effects of many common antibiotics. They must not be given penicillin or erythromycin.

There are normally good or beneficial bacteria (or flora, as veterinarians call them) in a guinea pig's intestines. When penicillin (and a few other less common antibiotics) is given to a guinea pig, certain bacteria die and one kind of bacteria grows abundantly. These changes cause diarrhea and even death in three to seven days. Death results if the guinea pig has a certain type of antibiotic-resistant flora in its intestines.

Tetracycline is a much safer antibiotic for an ill guinea pig.

PREGNANCY TOXEMIA
(Blood Poisoning)

This blood poisoning condition that occurs late in pregnancy comes on quickly and can result in death unless the guinea pig does give birth. It is brought on by obesity and stress during pregnancy.

It can be prevented in three ways. First, make sure the guinea pig does not become too fat. Second, she must receive good quality food while she is pregnant. Third, it is important to avoid stress while she is pregnant. Any stress that might cause her to stop eating is dangerous. One of the signs of toxemia is loss of appetite.

Remember that stress can be caused by a change in daily routine. The food, amount of attention, temperature, and noise should not change drastically.

A similar condition is seen in male guinea pigs that are obese. Again, stress is a major factor in this condition.

SALMONELLA

This is one of the most lethal, but fortunately uncommon, diseases of guinea pigs. The animal develops a fever and diarrhea and dies within two days. A breeder of guinea pigs would have to talk to a veterinarian about ridding his animals of the disease. Some animals could be carriers of the disease. The whole colony of guinea pigs might have to be euthanized.

Please note that this disease is rare. It is included for those guinea pig fanciers who want to know a little extra about potential problems.

SCURVY (Vitamin C Deficiency)

Guinea pigs need vitamin C or ascorbic acid added to their diet. Like people, they do not make their own vitamin C. Scurvy is the result of vitamin C deficiency.

Sailors used to develop scurvy on long ocean voyages. They did not have enough fresh fruit to provide them with enough vitamin C. Signs of scurvy are an unsteady gait or way of walking, pain when moving, and loss of condition. There may even be bleeding from the gums.

Scurvy can be prevented in guinea pigs by providing 1 to 3 mg of vitamin C for each 100 grams of body weight. That means about 20 mg of ascorbic acid in 100 ml of water for a two and a half pound guinea pig.

Guinea pig pellets do have vitamin C added, but its effectiveness is doubtful after eight to 12 weeks. The guinea pig's diet should therefore include vegetables and greens high in vitamin C.

WASTING DISEASE

This is the common name for an all too common guinea pig ailment. It is a terrible sign to a guinea pig owner or breeder. The guinea pig does seem to waste away. The animal drinks a lot of water. Its chin is usually wet, and its mouth often has a strong odor. The guinea pig drops weight, hunches up, loses condition, and gradually becomes weaker until death.

This is apparently a kidney disease that is very serious. Wasting disease, at this point, has been incurable.

A Last Word About T.L.C.

Sometimes people think there is a very serious medical problem with their pets when in reality the cause is non-medical. Guinea pigs are pretty sensitive animals. They are alarmed easily, respond quickly to noise and movement, and form attachments to human and animal companions. As a matter of fact, changes in the guinea pig's environment can cause changes in the guinea pig's behavior.

Usually when an animal begins to act differently, he is trying to tell you something. Cats are best known for their nonsocial behavior when a new kitten is brought into the household or when the furniture is moved. Fortunately, guinea pigs do not scratch furniture, hiss, or urinate on walls, but they do exhibit behavior changes when a major part

Tortoiseshell and white guinea pig.

of their everyday life changes.

Guinea pigs relish attention. They respond more to their human friend than people realize. Let me recount what happened to some guinea pigs. When a change occurred in their environment or daily routine, the guinea pigs began to exhibit highly unusual behavior. They leaped into the air, twisted, practically did flips, and had convulsions! They were suspected of having epilepsy.

When checked thoroughly by a veterinarian, however, there were no signs of epilepsy. Careful questioning revealed that there had been a change in each of the guinea pigs' lives. In one case the guinea pig's little girl friend had gone off to school for the first time. In another case the guinea pig was moved to a secluded area of the house where he was too isolated. When the owners began to pay attention to the guinea pig again, the peculiar behavior ceased.

Your guinea pig craves attention and will respond appropriately to your humane concern.

Breeding Guinea Pigs

Many people who now raise guinea pigs started out with just one wonderful pet guinea pig. If this one pet was such a dear little friend, then it must be wonderful to have many guinea pigs! More is not necessarily better. It depends on what you want, why you want that, and what is suitable for you and your lifestyle.

The answer to the first question of "What do you want?" may be "I want to raise guinea pigs." All right, but now we must honestly answer the question "Why?". If you want to raise guinea pigs just to have them around, think again. Remember that guinea pigs are living things that rely on people for all their needs. They must be fed, cleaned, and given attention, fresh water, and perhaps veterinary care. Unexpected expenses can arise.

If you want to raise guinea pigs because you like baby animals, please abandon that notion. Pets should live with people because the people are willing to be responsible. The pets must be cared for for their entire lifetime. A cute baby animal quickly grows into an adult. It still needs the same attention that it did as a baby. In the case of guinea pigs, this care may continue for about five or six years.

Now if after reading this you honestly know that you are willing to accept these responsibilities, you must still consider several more questions or angles.

What is suitable for your lifestyle? Do you have the space to house very many guinea pigs? If they are housed separately, each guinea pig needs a cage about 2 feet square. When the male is put into a cage with one or two females, you still will want them to have their own space later when the females give birth.

Do you have the facilities to store quantities of shavings and food? Do you have a convenient place to dispose of the soiled bedding? Is your selected space draft-free, warm enough in winter, and cool enough in summer?

What will you do with the baby guinea pigs? That is the bottom line. It will probably be impossible for you to keep all of the offspring. They must get good homes.

Anyone will take a cute baby animal, but they will not necessarily give it a good home. People tend to acquire on impulse. You might call it the desire to acquire. You know from reading this book that pets are a big responsibility. Too many people do not think of that when they see a cute baby guinea pig.

Breeding Guinea Pigs

Realize that you also may have difficulty letting your baby "leave the nest." Many conscientious owners want to be sure that the offspring will get the kind of care that they should receive. Once a guinea pig goes to a new home, it is not possible for you to make sure that someone always remembers to fill its water bottle, check for drafts, and handle it very gently. Because of this, you might have trouble giving up your baby guinea pigs. You should realize also that someone who quickly adopts a guinea pig may just as quickly lose interest in it and neglect it.

If, after giving a lot of consideration to these points, you do decide to go ahead and raise guinea pigs, then give a little thought to the purpose for which they are being raised.

Will these be just pets, or do you want to try for quality show guinea pigs? That means choosing a breed and learning a little about genetics. A good show guinea pig will probably be pedigreed. Pedigreed means there is a written record of the guinea pig's parents, grandparents, and great grandparents. Unless it is shown in a "Pet" category, the guinea pig will have to be a purebred: Its parents and relatives on the pedigree are all the same breed.

If you have decided to breed show-quality guinea pigs, you should start with good stock. Become knowledgeable about the breed you select. Visit guinea pig shows and observe the judging. If you have the chance, talk to the judge about what he or she looks for in a guinea pig. Also, spend plenty of time conversing with the people showing the guinea pigs, especially the people who win Best of Breed and Best Opposite Sex of Breed. The Best of Show is awarded to the guinea pig that comes nearest to the perfect standard.

Once you are comfortable with your knowledge of the breed, you should acquire a pair of good quality guinea pigs. They should conform to the breed standard for color and shape. Once you have some good guinea pigs, you can try to breed them.

Some people have the mistaken notion that guinea pigs are very prolific. That is not true. First of all, they usually have only three babies. Secondly, they may not be cooperative breeders. Despite what you read recommending all sorts of techniques to get your guinea pigs to breed, the fact is that they will mate when they feel like it!

The most successful method seems

Breeding Guinea Pigs

to be to put a male (one who is interested in the ladies) in a cage with two to six females. You can leave them together for several weeks.

Female guinea pigs are polyestrous, which means that they have "heat" cycles during the year. The cycle varies from every 13 to every 20 days. She is "in heat" actually for only about 15 hours. That is the time she can be bred. Like many rodents, guinea pigs also have a heat cycle right after they give birth.

Female guinea pigs may be able to conceive when they are five weeks old. The males usually become fertile when they are about eight to ten weeks old. It is obvious that the males and females must be separated fairly early when they are youngsters.

Female guinea pigs should be bred when they are about six months old. There is still a disunion of the pelvis then, and they should be bred before the pelvis fuses. This eliminates certain complications at birth. If a female is bred before she is five or six months old, however, it can stunt her growth and she may give birth to small and weak babies. Males should also be bred when they are six months old or older.

Although a male guinea pig may be placed with several females, males should not be together. Male guinea pigs will fight and perhaps even kill each other unless they were raised and kept together.

Once you think your female guinea pigs are bred, you may separate them from the male. The gestation period for guinea pigs is fairly long. It takes two months or about 63 days for the baby guinea pigs to be born. As the time approaches for the female to give birth she will start to take on the shape of a mandolin. It is extremely important that she receives good nutrition when she is pregnant. If she does not, both she and the youngsters will be affected.

When the mother gives birth, she should be in her own cage with a nestbox. She will use the nestbox for herself after the "pups" are born. Usually a litter of three or four is born. However, this could vary from one to six.

The young guinea pigs are born "ready to go." Their eyes are open (they open two weeks before they are born), they can hear, and they have all their hair. Their little ears stick straight up. Within half an hour they can be running around squeaking "Where are we now?!" Most rodents, and rabbits too, have a fairly short gestation time. Their young are born hairless, with their eyes closed, and are quite helpless. Guinea pigs

Breeding Guinea Pigs

develop inside the mother four weeks longer than do rabbits, which helps explain why they are so developed when they are born.

The babies will run in the cage and eat soft food (like lettuce) a few hours after they are born. The mother will spend most of her time in the nestbox. She lets the babies sleep elsewhere in the cage. If you have several females (sows) with litters at the same time, they can be kept together. A mothering sow will nurse any of the babies, even if they belong to someone else! The boar (male) should always be removed when there is a litter. He can be put back with the females after the babies are weaned.

The young should stay with their mother until they are 14 to 16 days old. They will have been eating pellets off and on for quite a while by then. They must be weaned by the time they are three weeks old or they can injure the mother's nipples.

Weigh the young when they are three weeks old. They should weigh about eight ounces. Any that weigh less than that should not be used for breeding later on, since they are probably not the healthiest. Keep a careful eye on them and let them go as pets only.

The guinea pigs will gain weight until they are 15 months old. An adult female will weigh about 30 to 32 ounces, a male about 32 to 42 ounces. Some particular lines or strains of guinea pigs will be much heavier than others.

Guinea pigs can be bred until they are about four years old. In commercial facilities (such as breeding laboratories) they will be used until they are two years old. The males may be used for only one year.

Guinea pigs learn everything from their mother. They learn to squeak for food, drink from a water bottle, and be afraid or cautious around people.

Normally baby guinea pigs will dash away from people, but as they grow older they become accustomed to people. Anyone who has handled guinea pigs knows that their first response when a hand reaches into their cage is to run. They dash and scurry around the cage. This quite often discourages the timid person, and when the guinea pig takes off, he usually jerks his hand back in alarm. The guinea pig sometimes seems to be playing a game of tag and the person is "it." Gentle handling and quietly cornering the scampering guinea pig seem to overcome the racing behavior. A pet guinea pig who is talked to a lot and receives gentle attention generally abandons this action.

Breeding Guinea Pigs

Anyway, this behavior seems to be learned from the mother! The mother guinea pig may teach her young to act like this just in case of danger. Orphaned baby guinea pigs do not exhibit this racing off. It is thus not a natural reaction against enemies but rather a learned action.

Orphaned babies also have to be taught by an ingenious owner how to drink from a water bottle. Usually tapping on the end of the bottle and placing the water drops on the guinea pig's mouth will give it the idea that water comes from that funny looking thing.

The notorious squeaking of guinea pigs is also a learned noise. Orphaned babies will eventually pick it up from other guinea pigs in adjacent cages. Like any language, they need to learn it from someone already fluent in it.

Multi-compartmented hutch equipped with removable partitions.

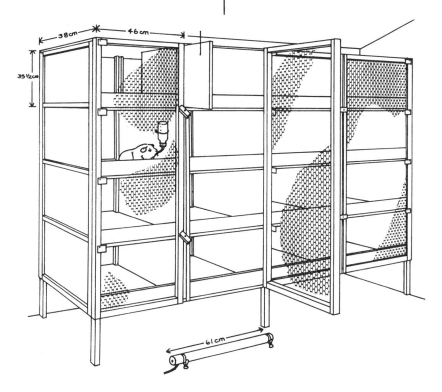

Breeding Guinea Pigs

Babies may also learn to barber from their mother. They may chew her hair or each other's. It does seem that if the parents are hair-chewing parents, then the babies will also chew. This is probably not a genetic behavior pattern; it is more likely to be a learned behavior that is cheerfully passed on, much to the distress of the owner if the guinea pigs are long-haired Peruvians and Silkies.

Peruvian guinea pig.

A type of hutch used by large-scale keepers of guinea pigs. The inset shows the type of information that should be recorded for controlled breeding results.

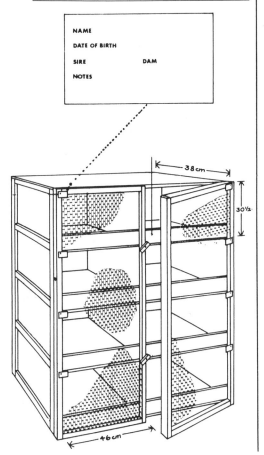

NAME

DATE OF BIRTH

SIRE   DAM

NOTES

38cm

30½

46cm

Simple Genetics

Anyone breeding guinea pigs will enjoy seeing the offspring of two adults that may be very different from one another. A little understanding of genetics can give you enjoyment and possibly success in breeding for certain characteristics.

Genetics is the study of heredity and the traits passed on from parents to offspring. Every trait or characteristic is determined by (at least) a pair of genes, which is where we get our word genetics. One gene comes from the father and one gene comes from the mother. There are many genes on each chromosome. Each guinea pig has

Breeding Guinea Pigs

64 chromosomes. They receive 32 from the father and 32 from the mother. The chromosomes have the code that tells the baby guinea pig what to look like.

Genes determine coat length, color, intensity of color, etc. Some genes are dominant and some are recessive. A dominant gene when combined with a recessive gene will mask the recessive gene. The animal will look like the dominant trait. For example, the gene for short-hair is dominant over the gene for long-hair. If a pure Abyssinian (short-haired) is mated with a pure Peruvian (long-haired), the babies will all be short-haired. They will have short-hair because they will all receive one short-hair gene from the Abyssinian parent and one long-hair gene from the Peruvian parent. The dominant short-hair gene will mask the long-hair gene. If one of the babies is long-haired, you know that the Abyssinian had some Peruvian in its past; it had a long-haired gene that it passed on to its offspring.

Here is a written example of what happened. A capital letter represents a dominant gene and a small letter represents a recessive gene. We will let H = short-haired and h = long-haired. The pure Peruvian (hh) crossed with a pure Abyssinian (HH) will produce short-haired babies (Hh).

HH x hh = Hh babies.

If that Abyssinian-looking (genetically mixed or heterozygous) guinea pig (Hh) is crossed with a pure Peruvian (hh), the offspring will look like this: Hh x hh = Hh and hh babies, with both short-haired (Hh) and Peruvian (hh) offspring. Remember, the baby receives one gene from each parent.

In guinea pigs, short-haired is dominant to long-haired. It also seems that the rough-coat is dominant over the smooth-coat. If you breed a rough-coated Abyssinian (with the rosettes) with a smooth-coated American, the babies will have rough-coats with rosettes of some sort. A guinea pig may look like an Abyssinian (SS, the dominant coat) but carry the American smooth-coat (ss) gene. If two of these are bred (Ss), an American may result. This explains why a breeder can breed two Abyssinians and have an American baby guinea pig. One may get a smooth-coated Silkie from breeding two Peruvians that each carry one recessive smooth-coat gene.

Certain colors are dominant to others. You may want to talk to other guinea pig breeders to learn what they have found concerning color dominance. For instance, black

Breeding Guinea Pigs

Dutch-marked guinea pig.

is dominant over the color red and possibly tortoise shell (red and black patches) as well.

The Odds are 3:1

In our genetic study, we realize certain traits are dominant. A guinea pig may be pure for the trait or may have the recessive gene, too, which is masked or does not show up. That case (like Hh) is called heterozygous. The individual is called a hybrid.

When you breed two individuals which look like the dominant trait but are not pure for the dominant trait, you can expect the following.

The odds are that they will produce three dominant-looking babies and one recessive baby. Two of the dominant-looking offspring will carry the recessive gene (heterozygous). One of them will be pure for the dominant trait. This is one of Mendel's laws of inheritance. A monk named Mendel figured out this genetic ratio using peas in the early 1800's. You will find guinea pigs are more interesting.

Mother (Hh) mated with Father (Hh)

Genes from Father (columns); Genes from Mother (rows)

	H	h
H	HH	Hh
h	Hh	hh

The HH will be the pure dominant.
The Hh will look dominant.
The hh will be the pure recessive.

Some gene combinations may produce weak animals. One such case concerns genes involved in roans. A roan has a mixture of white and colored hair. Two roans can produce unhealthy babies, so it is best to breed a roan with another color guinea pig. If breeders can determine which combinations are unsuccessful in producing healthy animals, than they can help prevent and eliminate some problems.

Breeding guinea pigs can be fun and very interesting. Just remember

Breeding Guinea Pigs

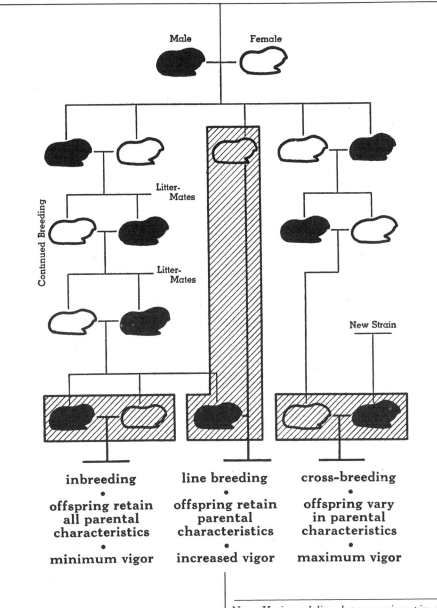

Male Female

Continued Breeding

Litter-Mates

Litter-Mates

New Strain

inbreeding
•
offspring retain
all parental
characteristics
•
minimum vigor

line breeding
•
offspring retain
parental
characteristics
•
increased vigor

cross-breeding
•
offspring vary
in parental
characteristics
•
maximum vigor

Note: Horizontal lines between guinea pigs indicate matings; vertical lines indicate offspring.

Breeding Guinea Pigs

Although sturdily constructed, this four-tier hutch has a major fault: it allows ventilation only at the front.

Cavy Breeders Association (Box 180a, Rt. RD2, Zionsville, PA 18092) can supply you with information about cavy or guinea pig shows and cavy breeders' associations in your area.

Portable cages without bottoms are useful for protecting guinea pigs placed outdoors on a lawn during good weather.

A portable outdoor cage should be light in weight for easy carrying, but it should be strong enough to keep other animals away from the guinea pigs.

the responsibility involved in finding good homes for the animals. You might want to discover which colors and breeds are a challenge to develop at show quality in your area. This might be the type of guinea pig on which you would like to concentrate.

To learn more about guinea pig breeds and colors, write to The American Rabbit Breeders Association, P.O. Box 426, Bloomington, IL 61701. You can request information on membership and their *Standard of Perfection*. The A.R.B.A. and the American

Suggested Reading

GUINEA PIGS: A COMPLETE INTRODUCTION
By Margaret Elward
Hardcover: ISBN 0-86622-366-5; TFH CO-038
Softcover: ISBN 0-86622-383-5; TFH CO-038S

Guinea pigs make great pets if you know how to care for them properly. This book will teach the reader everything he needs to know about caring for these lovable little mammals. It covers every topic of importance—including housing, breeding, feeding, health care, taming and training, genetics, and showing—in specific yet easy to understand detail. In addition, this book is heavily illustrated with 116 full-color photos and 19 drawings.

GUINEA PIGS
By Kay Ragland
ISBN 0-87666-925-9
KW-016

Completely illustrated with full-color photographs and drawings, this eye-catching volume provides detailed sections on guinea pig maintenance and specifics on color varieties, ailments, and training.

A STEP-BY-STEP BOOK ABOUT GUINEA PIGS
By Anmarie Barrie
Hardcover: ISBN 0-86622-916-7; TFH SK-013X
Softcover: ISBN 0-86622-450-5; TFH SK-013

Magnificently colorful book containing practical, easy to read advice on keeping guinea pigs as pets. Completely illustrated with full-color photography and with humorous full-color cartoons.

BEGINNER'S GUIDE TO GUINEA PIGS
By Tom Wilkie
ISBN 0-86622-304-5
TFH T-105

The definitive beginner's guide to the world of guinea pigs. Perfect for children, this little book is completely illustrated with full-color photographs.

BREEDING GUINEA PIGS
By Jennifer Axelrod
ISBN 0-86622-827-6
TFH KW-073

This book tells you everything you need to know about breeding guinea pigs, with special emphasis placed on genetics and selection. Contains 51 full-color and 42 black and white photographs.

Index